RE·SIL·IENT
/RƏˈZILĒƏNT/

You Can Begin Again

Deborius Greene

NEW YORK

Dedication

I would like to dedicate this book to the Holy Spirit who is the Author, Originator and Finisher of my book

Keep your eyes on Jesus, who both began and finished this race we're in. Study how he did it. Because he never lost sight of where he was headed —that exhilarating finish in and with God—he could put up with anything along the way: Cross, shame, whatever. And now he's there, in the place of honor, right alongside God.
Hebrews 12:2 (The Message Bible)

Deborius Greene

Resilience Defined .....

Resilience is the ability to bounce back from difficult times in life. Resilience comes from the lessons and skills we absorb as we grow up and as we face all of our difficulties whatever they are.

Table Of Contents

Foreword

Dear Reader,

We are truly elated to write this foreword on behalf of Deborius Greene. Deborius is an authentic, resilient, and powerful woman and we are simply awed by her tenacity and ability to endure the challenges of life with grace and strength. Min. Greene joined our church many years ago and her gifts and talents were clearly seen. Her ability to pray fervently and with such passion, conveyed to us all that God's hand was on her life. Upon meeting her and genuinely blessed by her life story, her love of Christ and his people helped us to understand that purpose and destiny was indeed her guide.

It is not easy to stand in dark and perilous times proclaiming the truth and hope of Christ, but she does so through her actions and the spirit of her testimony. In this book she is choosing to share her journey through life's challenges with her readers in a very relatable way. It takes bravery to reveal the most intimate scenes of one's life. However, Min. Greene does it with grace and complete transparency; there is no holding back when it comes to seeing how she effortlessly learns from her mistakes, utilizing those lessons to find her breakthroughs.

We have witnessed her rise from the ashes of her circumstances, which has resulted in her deep conversion and call to action. Conversely, have also witnessed her live unapologetically following and seeking Christ no matter the obstacles or outcomes. Her passionate prayers given for families, community, and a clarion call for the church to become an unspotted bride is exemplary! To know her is to marvel at the boldness in which she intercedes for families, friends, and communities alike. As you read every page, may the grace and strength expressed in her life, effortlessly become a part of yours. We welcome you to witness her journey and with every chapter, feel your faith get challenged, altered but ultimately grow for the better.

Our Love and Faith,
Dr. Phyllis F. Rodges
Bishop James G. Rodges

Foreword

John 12:24 (ESV): Truly, truly, I say to you, unless a grain of wheat falls into the earth and dies, it remains alone; but if it dies, it bears much fruit.

John 12:24 invites us to die to ourselves, to our selfish ambitions, and to our fears. In a way it's saying that we decrease daily for Jesus Christ to increase in us. By embracing this call, we find that it is only in dying to ourselves that we can truly live and experience the abundant life and power of our Lord Jesus Christ and all it offers.

Pastor Deborius is the epitome of brokenness and resilience being tested and tried by fire in ministries in which she served. She is Deborah (in Judges Chapters 4 and 5) of our time whom GOD recognizes and endorses to continue to minister to the heirs of salvation for the end time to populate heaven and de-populate hell.

I met her in August 1995 while serving at Living faith Church in Mt. Vernon New York. As I left the church to serve at Mountain Of Fire and Miracles Ministries where I became the Pastor at The New York City Manhattan Mountain of Fire at Times Square, I still maintained our relationship because souls like her are difficult to come by. Pastor Deborius was one of the five Pastors under me as the Pastor in charge of prayer warriors. She served with humility, honesty and love but above all she hates sin so perfectly (soundness, integrity, and maturity). She was my right hand Pastor with honesty, diligence and punctuality regardless of the distance from her home in Brooklyn, New York to New York City Manhattan traveling on public transportation. It gives me joy to recommend this book to everyone and it will edify you abundantly.

Prophetess Deborah Bridget Bennett
Divine Intervention Fire Int'l Ministries NYC

Foreword

As you began to read this book, like the Holy Bible its filled with life experiences that will cause you to remember your own. Many of our lives have been filled with mental and emotional pain, along with disappointments, and spiritual paralysis, that have influenced who we have become.

It is through the chaotic whirlwinds of her own life that Evangelist Greene shares her testimony of how she survived and conquered.

Like the Bible, this book is inspired by the Holy Spirit, and will help bring deliverance to those of us who need to know that our God is the God of all flesh, and that there is nothing too hard for Him.

Pastor Julius L. McNabb Sr

This woman who I knew not, yet we stepped into divine destiny when we met for the first time. There was a powerful anointing as we embraced; that is directly connected with the ancestral bloodline of her grandmother. And I knew that destiny had met purpose!

Evangelist Deborius, the woman I have come to know, is a Prayer Warrior, Woman of Faith, a Servant, who throughout her personal tragedies has developed a more than a conqueror spirit. Yet, her desire is to be an instrument used by God to bring healing and change to the life of others. Although the crushing has been great, the restoration has been dunamis, (explosive)!

Lady Denise McNabb

WE validate the authenticity of her calling, and pray that you will receive every word, every sentence, every paragraph with an open heart and a porous spirit. In doing so, may the wind of the Holy Spirit bring healing to every wounded area of your life, for we know that Evangelist Deborius has heard from God!

God's Kingdom Church
godskingdomchurchgkc@gmail.com

Introduction

My name is Deborius Eugenia Greene and I was born in Savannah, Georgia September 5th, 1950, at this time I had two siblings Orpheus Eugene Holsey Jr. and Nathaniel Eugene Holsey. We grew up without our father Orpheus Eugene Holsey presence in the house. Our mother QuoVadis was a young mother trying to survive raising three kids the best she knew. One day our mother was on the phone and my brother Nathaniel (bubba) and I was playing in the kitchen, there was a pot of hot water on the stove boiling. The stove was unbalance and something attracted our attention, like kids we wanted what we saw. I got a chair and climbed up to the stove and reached for whatever it was and the pot of boiling water fell and splashed on my left arm and my brothers back and shoulder. We hollered so loud my mother came running and saw us on the floor. She panicked and screamed as she saw our skin melting from our bodies. I don't remember what happen after she saw us but I could hear her crying and my great grand mother was there with her home remedies. I was just a frighten kid who was scared because I thought if I hadn't climbed up on the stove this would not have happened. I was laying on the bed with my brother who was on his stomach crying and sniffling, hollering it hurts. I was crying also it hurts but I felt guilty and so bad for my brother when I saw his back and shoulder and he couldn't lay in another position for months it traumatized me and my brother. I blocked out what had happened to me. My family said we were around 11-12 years old when this happen. Even up until today when we talk about it we don't know what we were trying to get over the stove. It was trauma that cause me to forget what it was like to grow up as a happy normal kid. Not only did I have a physical scar I was left with internal scars.

What is trauma?

Carol Ann Faigin, Ph.d. licensed psychologist said "trauma is a psychological response to an experience or an event that is deeply disturbing or distressing mentally and emotionally reliving the experience or loss lead to isolation or avoidance of triggers. intense or unpredictable emotions (sadness, anger, shame, guilt, despair). Physical symptoms (being on edge or nausea, headaches, change view of oneself and others world), including that which we hold sacred, acrimony, trust, safety, power/control, intimacy and esteem."

When God is ready to heal your trauma he will bring it back to your remembrance and cut it to the root of the problem(s) and take the sting out of it to begin your healing process. There are so many people in the bible who went through challenging times such as Job (Job 1:20-21, Job 10:1-4), David (Psalms 142:1-2), Moses (Exodus 15:25), and Peter (Mark 14:72), John (21:15-25). If you are going through difficult times or feeling scared, with the help of our Lord and Savior Jesus Christ you can make it to the other side with the Holy Spirit as your guide. I have learned that with God all things are possible (Matthew 15:26).

It is rather funny that people look at me as "I got It going on","having it altogether' or "at the top of my game". Little do they know that deep within me is a sense of insecurity that comes from my chIldhood. It is o'kay because I realize lots of people grew up with me had some of the same problems I had. All of us have issues in our lives but that didn't change the reality that I felt insecure. As a child I never quite figured out how to relate to people. I felt like I didn't fit in or that people liked or wanted me as a friend because of my scar. When I was about 4 or 5 years old my oldest brother Nathaniel Holsey and I was playing in the kitchen and my mother was in the living room on the phone. My mother was boiling hot water with grits on the stove and the stove was unleveled. Something over the stove attracted our attention and we wanted it like most children who are curious. To this day we don't remember what it was. I got a chair and climbed up on the stove and it tilted causing the hot water and grits to splatter on my brothers shoulder and back as well as my left arm. We hollered and cried so loud my mother came running and saw us laying in the hot water. Our skin was melting off the bone. I could hear her crying and screaming. I don't remember what happened after that but the next person I saw was my great grandmother we call "Momma". She was there with her home remedies. I was lying next to my brother and I could hear him sniffing from crying and saying it hurts. I was crying also it hurts but I felt so bad for my brother when I saw his back and shoulders. He couldn't lay in another position for months. This trauma caused me to forget what it was like to grow up as a normal kid. I felt guilty for what happened to my brother because if I had never got the chair none of this would have happened.

Re·sil·ient
/rə'zilēənt/

I learned when God is ready to heal your scars he will bring it back to your remembrance. My brother and I were traumatized by this accident mentally, emotionally and physically. Every time I would look at my arm all I could see was ugliness. As I grew up in my adolescent and teenage years I grew up wIth a complex. I saw myself in the mirror as a girl scarred for life. I would look in the mirror at myself and say who will want you as his girlfriend, nobody will marry you when they see that scar. I hid my scar for years. You see all my friends had beautIful skin, no scars on their arms or body that I could see. I was born in Savannah, Georgia where the temperature was 95-100 degrees in the summer. No one noticed that I was wearing long sleeves. The other girls were wearing short sleeves blouses, halter tops looking cute and attractive to all the boys. I could only imagine the fun they were having. I would go home and cry myself to sleep all night, hating myself for having this scar asking why this had to happen to me? I wanted to tell someone about my scars, I wanted a friend. I needed a friend. In many ways they were everything I wanted to be. I would go shopping at the clothing store and see beautIful dresses that were short sleeves and wished I had the courage enough to wear them but it only became a dream. Even though they were my friends they didn't know my secret. I felt Insecure. As time went on I got used to hiding my scar and dated boys but they never knew I had a scar. In Junior High School I had a best friend who I thought was my true friend. We both attended Alfred E Beach high school and joined the majorettes. I met this handsome guy name Oscar Alphonso Greene, Jr in elementary school and to my surprise was in the band in High School as well. Oscar was also known as "Ballie". His parents had two cleaners, a club and real estate. As time went on I discovered my best friend was also attracted to Oscar .

First time showing burn on my arm without covering it up

Re·sil·ient
/rə'zilēənt/

He was very nice and popular with all the girls and they were attracted to him as well. We became friends and later dated. Inspite of all the girls that were attracted to him he chose me, the one with the scar. Life is hard and sometimes it will knock you off your feet. It is on the journey to discover who you are the devil will come to distract you and your plans. What we want to do can collapse, Proverbs 16:9 says "A man's heart deviseth his way: but the Lord directeth his steps. The Lord had already established who I am and what I would go through to become before the foundation of the world. My journey begins after the scar on my arm. I suffered in silence with low self-esteem and self-worth. I struggled to see myself as beautiful. Every time I would look at my arm all I could see was ugliness, I did not know Jesus as my savior and how much He loved me with my scar. I did not know he thought I was worth dying for. I hid the scar for years. Isn't it strange how we can be around people day after day, week after week, month after month and sometimes years and don't know them. You don't see their pains or know they are hurting. We sit next to people in church services Sunday after Sunday, bible study after bible study, revival after revival, sometimes one conference after another conference and never fellowship because you allow the spirit of fear to prevent you from the move of the HOLY SPIRIT so you can be used to minister to their hurt, or give a word of encouragement. As I was saying I wanted to tell them and show them my scars, but the question always comes, would they still be my friend or reject me?

Were they going to laugh at me, gossip to each other about my ugly scars? Even in church who can you trust to tell your real secrets. It is sad to say but church folks can be unloving, unkind and evil. That is why people don't give their real testimonies, because church folks will use it to scorn and reject you, push you aside instead of embracing you with the love of Jesus Christ. I decided to go have plastic surgery on my arm, after three surgeries the scar is still there. I thank GOD for my deliverance and healing. The scar no longer hurts, except for the memory. I remember how it got there. I remember the pain that I went through when the scar was made. I wish I could forget it, but the reminder is still there. God took the sting of the scar away. If I didn't tell you my story most of you would never have known because I covered my wound for over fifty years, but today the HOLY Spirit said "Show You My Scars". The scars are there to remind me not to make the same mistake again. Mistakes can be good if we learn from them. The problem is most of the time we make the same mistakes over and over again. The burn arm knows not to go too close to the fire. It may have some burned scar tissues on it, but it also has some experience that the unscarred arm does not have. This scar reminds me that an arm is not useless just because it has a scar.

God has a plan for the scars and he is using it today for his glory. "For I know the plans I have for you", declares the Lord," plans to prosper you and not to harm you, plans to give you a hope and a future." (Jeremiah 29:11 NIV)

As time went by I got pregnant in the 12th grade my senior year and was able to graduate with my class. My son Oscar Alphonso Greene III was born November 18th, 1968. A few months later I was married, young and naive. I had no idea what it was like to be a mother or a wife. Oscar's parents gave us a house to live in as a family. My husband became a fireman and would be gone for 24-48 hrs at a time required of his job. My best friend and I would talk and a lot of the conversation was about my marriage. I started getting phone calls from another woman about my husband and I would share it with her. I found out she was the one calling me on those phone calls and having an affair with my husband. I felt betrayed, she had broke our trust and here I go again with another emotional and spiritual injury. Remember I am not born again yet. It was hard for me to forgive her I knew from going to church that is what God calls us to do. I was in pain, angry, and I hated her. I had self pity and self contempt to deal with. The saddest part of betrayal is it almost always come from those you trust or love. I said from that day I found out I would never trust again. I never let anyone get that close to me or my relationship with my man because of that experience. I still don't let people into my space unless I am led by the Holy Spirit. Eventually for my own good and the good of my mental and emotional health I had to forgive the persons (my husband and my so called best friend) I now know how David felt when he said in Psalms 41:9 :"yea, mine own familiar friend, in whom i trusted, which did eat of my bread, hath lifted up his heel against me". Everybody in town knew about the relationship I felt violated and ashamed for being so naive I knew I could not live in Savannah anymore and be happy. Two years later I divorced him.

Re·sil·ient
/rə'zilēənt/

One day I was at a club and met this guy who was traveling from New York, and later found out his brother was dating my so called best friend sister. We started dating and he would come back and forth from New York. He said he loved me and wanted to marry me, I said yes because I saw him as my escape out of Savannah. We got to the courthouse in South Carolina and something said don't do it. I never heard this voice before and I had a nervous stomach, so I listened to that voice and told him lets wait until we get to New York. He was disappointed but we still went to New York anyway.

Re·sil·ient
/rə'zilēənt/

Questions

Where did your journey begin?

What circumstances put you in the situation
you are facing?

What you are doing is this thing going to add value
to your future ?

Am I making decisions based on my emotions or something
that will have longevity?

What difference will the decisions make in my life or
someone else's life?

Why did I waste my time judging myself by the words of
man, and not by the word of God?

Take a good look at yourself in the mirror.
What do you see?

"May the Lord bless you and protect you. May the LORD smile
on you and be gracious to you. May the lord show you His favor
and give you His peace"
Numbers 6:24-26 (NLT)

I love you!

Re·sil·ient
/rəˈzilēənt/

Journaling

Re·sil·ient
/rə'zilēənt/

Journaling

Re·sil·ient
/rə'zilēənt/

Journaling

One of the most valuable experiences I have learned in my Christian journey is that people feel relatable to you and I feel closer to them when we stop trying to impress each other. People want relationships with those who are real, genuine, compassionate, loving, kind, trustworthy, loyal, supportive and not judgemental. We are all in need of surgery. We all have wounds and issues. All scars tell a story. As you begin reading this chapter the HOLY SPIRIT has already begun the prepping for surgery. Today we are going to symbolize your space as the hospital's emergency room. We all have been set up with a divine appointment by the CEO, the person who controls the operations and gives the final decisions and strategies in every area of your body. The CEO is Jesus Christ,"The stone which the builders rejected, the same is become the head of the corner: this is the Lord's doing, and it is marvelous in our eyes?" (Matthew 21:42) Many deliverance will take place in this room today. The surgeon in charge is the "Holy Spirit". You are helpless without him,"for the letter killeth, but the spirit giveth life."(II Corinthians 3:6) There will be heart transplants, birthing, deliverance, old wounds gutted out to be healed and transformation will take place. Now that you are admitted the first thing you must do is go through preparation. So before we go any further look at yourself in the mirror and say ,"Take the Mask Off", take it off so I can see who you really are. As you begin to peel the first layer off, it's going to hurt, it will be painful because it is rooted and grounded in you. If you got to cry, then cry, if you want to holler, call on Jesus. Whatever it takes, peel it off. Psalms 57:2 says "I will cry unto God most high; unto God that performeth all things for me".

Re·sil·ient
/rə'zilēənt/

This is key in understanding God's purpose for your life. As God speal His truth over us through his word about the scars and the healing on He can do, remember "faith without works is dead" (James 2:17) and you choices and actions really matter. Someone is reading this book with smile on their face but God knows there is an issue in your life, there a things that you are dealing with but our God is going to meet every nee and answer every prayer. He knows what you are going through and H cares. We need to understand that we are not on this earth b happenstance or coincidence but because God has predestined us sin before the foundation of the world. Everyone has scars they hav experienced in their life. Some are very obvious, some are in more privat places, some are minor like a cut will usually heal and leave a mark an gradually fade over time. Some of them inside and some outside. In ever case each one represents a bad experience. The Bible says, "Neither there any creature that is not manifest in his sight: but all things a naked and opened unto the eyes of him with whom we have to dc (Hebrews 4:13). Take your hands and peel another layer off. "Show M Your Scars". What are scars? A scar is a wound that is healed. It is nc infected or festered. It is healed, and it has left behind some evidence c the trauma we have experienced. Scars of addictions, like drug gambling or pornography. Maybe it's chocolate, coffee, soap opera: video games. Regardless of their form, addictions leave scars. Some c you have marks on your body that are the result of sin. Sin is painfu you can enjoy the "...pleasures of sin for a season;"(Hebrews 11:25b)

Many times you don't even notice the scars until they have destroyed all or a part of your life. There are scars where physical pain has been inflicted which is more serious. They are called secret scars, you can't see them, they are hidden until you act out because of the hurt, the pain, disappointments and rejections. Some scars we cause on ourselves because of disobedience to God and some scars were done intentionally to anesthetize the pain. It's so easy to hold on to feelings of resentment, anger and bitterness over wrongs that have been done to you. We make excuses for harboring scars of unforgiveness in our hearts, scars are like a poison or an infection that slowly kills before we realize what's wrong. Many people when they are hurting on the inside try to put the best smile out front, they wear the best outfits, you know how we do ,we've been told to "fake it until you make it", hurting but bleeding, praising but dying, want people to think you "got it all together", when really you are "bleeding internally". It's time to stop faking and pretending and be real. You must forgive, it is for your own benefit. You must let go, refuse to hold on to the past ,let the person or persons off the hook. Let go of old habits and renew your mind. Paul said in (Romans 12:2) "And be not conformed to this world: but be ye transformed by the renewing of your mind, that ye may prove what is that good, and acceptable, and perfect, will of God". As God reveals to you the areas in your life where you need deliverance say 'Yes', LORD. You must be willing to empty yourself, you must be willing to surrender your will to God as JESUS surrendered his will to the father by saying, "Nevertheless not my will, but thine, be done." (Luke 22:42) You must die to your flesh and kill your flesh before your flesh kills you.

Let the Holy Spirit help you peel this next layer off. This emptying of self is a continual process. There are all types of ways to get scars, accidents, surgical cuts, war wounds, athletic, scars from bad marriages, divorces and many wrong relationships. Sometimes life has a hold on you. Everywhere you turn there is one thing after another. There are things in our heart we don't even know are there until we go through something. The Bible says in (Jeremiah 17:9) "The heart is deceitful above all things, and desperately wicked: Who can know it? It is the Lord who judges and changes the heart. It takes God to look into your heart and root out everything that should not be there.

You may be reading this book saying "I Don't need deliverance". Believers need deliverance because their souls were not born again when you were saved; our souls need deliverance and healing of past wounds and strongholds. If you will allow the Holy Spirit to use the hammer of his word and cut you He will show you the real you on the inside. Get in his presence, fast and pray, He will open up your eyes and show you your ugliness, He will show you the anger, the pride, hatred, prejudice. Oh yes he will. If you take a look deep down on the inside you will see the jealousy, your rebelliousness, your rejection, past wounds, He will show you your scars from your childhood and the strongholds that have you bound.

We all need to take a trip to the Potter's House. That is what he told Jeremiah:

"Arise, and go down to the potter's house, and there I will cause thee to hear my words (Jeremiah 18:2)."

Re·sil·ient

/rə'zilēə nt /

Put yourself on the potter's wheel and let the Lord break you, mold you again into another vessel. Lift your voice and say "Heal me, O LORD, and I shall be healed; save me, and I shall be saved: for thou art my praise (Jeremiah 17:14)" I am so glad that we serve a God that heals. He is a great physician, Jehovah-Rapha our God. I don't know what wounds that are open in your life, but fear not, "The Lord said to Jeremiah,"Is there no balm in Gilead; is there no physician there? why then is not the health of the daughter of my people recovered? (Jeremiah 8:22)" There is a balm in Gilead, a spiritual medicine that is able to heal a sin -sick soul.

Re·sil·ient
/rə'zilēə nt /

Questions

Think about it, scars are reminders of something.

1. What does your scars remind you of?

I have scars to remind me everyday of how much God loves me and has a purpose and plan for my scars and me.

2. Do you have scars?

3. Are you able to thank God for your scars?

4. You may be going through a trial in your life today and don't understand why.

What trials are you going through that make you think you are not going to make it to your destiny?

Remember the heroes of the Bible:

Jesus had scars. Isaiah 53.
Paul - 2 Corinthians 11:24-25
Job - Job 1:8-22, Job 2:7-8

I love you!

Re·sil·ient
/rə'zilēənt/

Journaling

Re·sil·ient
/rə'zilēənt/

Journaling

Re·sil·ient
/rə'zilēənt/

Journaling

Chapter 3
Transformation In The Wilderness

Here I am in the 'The Big Apple ' New York, New York on a hot summer day in 1971. I had never seen buildings so high and so many people like ants running all over the streets. I wonder to myself where are they going? Car horns blowing and everybody is in a hurry. Why am I here? I had no family members in New York. I'm broken, hurt, confused, mad, angry and I am bitter. What a mess I was and I had no idea that God was going to use all that in my wilderness experience. Yet, this place was the beginning of why I had to go through what I went through so God could get the glory out of my life and use me to be a blessing to thousands. Because of my pain I was not going to let anybody get close to me again. My Relationship didn't last long with him because my mind, spirit and emotions had been crushed. I eventually ended the relationship and got a job to become independent. I got into another relationship and thought this is the one I needed in my life who would love me for me. I found out he was no different from the others. I became a needy person looking for love in all the wrong places. A needy person has an odor that attracts those who know you are desperate for acceptance, insecure and need someone to validate you. I started living a promiscuous lifestyle. I came into every relationship wounded and broken. I vowed "I would hurt you before you hurt me." I still didn't know I needed to have a relationship with Jesus and that He was the answer to all of my problems. I found myself doing things I never imagined that could have brought me to my death but God didn't allow it to consume me because He had a plan for my life.

Re·sil·ient
/rə'zilēənt/

One day after partying all night and sniffing cocaine I found myself on the floor. My heart was palpitating and I thought I was going to die but I could hear my grandmother's voice saying when you get into trouble call on the name of Jesus. I called the name Jesus and I said "IF YOU" save me I will serve you for the rest of my life" I know today it is a cliche because they say that is what they all say but some of us say it and really mean it" I DID". I never went back to doing any kind of drugs from that day. I thought that I could live a better life but I soon found out when I got into another relationship that there were other demons in me I had to deal with. I needed an inside job and only Jesus could deliver me and make me whole. My life was crazy. I was still looking for love in all the wrong places because I still didn't surrender my Life to Jesus Christ. One day my neighbor Clara invited me to her church and I kept saying I was coming. She never stopped asking me to come with her to church and hear the word of the Lord. She talked about God's love for me. One day I said yes I will go to church and I did.I didn't know that God was setting me up for transformation and a deeper relationship with Him. The church was Pilgrim Church and the Pastor was the late Archbishop Roy E. Brown in Brooklyn, New York.The church was packed with people of all ages and the man of God spoke a message that God had tailored made just for me. I thought that my neighbor told him my business but I learned later in my walk with Christ that it was the " Holy Ghost" who convicted me. On November 18th 1985 I gave my life to Jesus Christ.

Re·sil·ient

/rə'zilēənt/

I have not been perfect but I am striving everyday for perfection. I realize that I had to go through in order to be effective in life and ministry. I know what it is to show mercy because I am a recipient of God's mercy. I learned to show mercy but never at the expense of truth. I believe that people and the church are hurting from the lack of mercy today. Sadly many non-believers and christians today have broken hearts, affliction of the mind, emotions, thoughts and spirit of a person. These scars or wounds could have come from people, places, situations and things. The words of a gossiper and a so-called friend can also cause scars or wounds. I had to be healed myself and be delivered and set free of a wounded spirit. The heart of God is for the people. The Lord Jesus came to "bind up the broken hearted" (Isaiah 61:1, 30:26, Job 5:18, 28:11; Ezekiel 34:4,16; Hosea 6:1; Luke 10:34). I am reminded by GOD'S LOVE to remember my own sinful condition before God healed my own wounds and scars, to be compassionate, patient and discern the areas in people's lives that need healing. Since the same HOLY SPIRIT that was upon Christ to bind up the brokenhearted and proclaim liberty to the captives and heal the bruised (Isaiah 61:1; Luke 4:18) is now upon me I must minister in this way to the needy.

My prayer for you is that God uses you to bring people that are brokenhearted to the healing love and forgiveness of Jesus Christ.

Re·sil·ient
/rə'zilēənt/

Questions

When God takes you into the wilderness there
are many challenges.

1. What did it take for you to survive the wilderness?

2. How did God transform your heart in the wilderness?

3. Why is your wilderness experience important?

I love you!

Re·sil·ient
/rə'zilēənt/

Journaling

Re·sil·ient
/rə'zilēənt/

Journaling

Re·sil·ient

/rə'zilēənt/

Journaling

Chapter 4
Can I Testify?

Ladies and gentlemen I don't look like what I've been through. I got some scars but I am healed. I am a proof producer that the word of God works. I am righteously proud of my deliverance and healing. If I didn't tell my story most of you would never have known because I covered my wound for over fifty years. I was thinking while writing this chapter of Jesus Christ and the wounds he bore for the sins of the world. His scars in his flesh were a sign of his love and our victory. Death could not hold him down his blood cries out and is heard "O death, where is thy sting? O grave, where is thy victory? (1 Corinthian 15:55)". His wounds were his proof to us that we serve a God who knows our pain. "For we have not a high priest which cannot be touched with the feelings of our infirmities; but was in all points tempted like as we are, yet without sin (Hebrew 4:15)". Perhaps if the scars or wounds were not there we would forget the sacrifice he made for us. His wounds tell us that all who choose to live Godly for him will suffer, "Yea, and all that will live godly in Christ Jesus shall suffer persecution (2 Timothy 3:12)". Your family may turn their backs on you when you make a commitment to live holy, and call you crazy, at the job you may be overlooked for promotion, church folks they will do you wrong, you will get pushed to the curb and left for dead. The wounds of Christ teach us that suffering is necessary. "No Cross NO Crown", nobody will ever know the tremendous price that has been paid in my 38 years of salvation. It hasn't been easy. I've been misunderstood, lied on, cheated and mistreated, talked about and rejected. Many times the attacks have been so heavy I felt like giving up but I couldn't because God wouldn't let me. I realized the calling of God on my life and the price Jesus paid. I have no choice.

Re·sil·ient
/rə'zilēənt/

My life is no longer my own, Peter replied, "Master, to whom would we go? You have the words of real life, eternal life. We've already committed ourselves, confident that you are the Holy One of God. (John 6:68-69)". Yes you will get tired and you will have some scars. "For I reckon that the sufferings of this present time are not worthy to be compared with the glory which shall be revealed in us. (Roman 8:18)". My question to you is, "Are you willing to pay the price?" No matter what the cost, will you be willing to suffer for Christ's sake? Regardless of what they taught you there is a price to pay. I want you to put your hands on your heart and be real with GOD and ask him to "Create in me a clean heart, O God; and renew a right spirit within me. (Psalms 51:10)" Wash my heart Lord, "Purge me with hyssop, and I shall be clean: wash me, and I shall be whiter than snow. (Psalms 51:7)". Ask God to purify me, sanctify me. I'm tired of myself. Let God deliver your soul, and let him wash your heart today. Tell the Lord I want to be Holy. If you are sincere in your prayers, lift your hands and surrender to God and receive your deliverance. It is time to take the mask off. The hour is late and Jesus is coming soon. Our major concern should no longer be the cares of this world, our own selfish desires and goals but we should be preparing ourselves for his coming and winning souls into the kingdom of GOD. I cannot end this chapter without this last remark. O sinner man you may say my scars are too many. Jesus is saying to you today, "Come unto me, all ye that labor and are heavy laden, and I will give you rest. Take my yoke upon you, and learn of me: for I am meek and lowly in heart: and ye shall find rest unto your souls. For my yoke is easy, and my burden is light. (Matthew 11:28-30) "

Re·sil·ient

/rə'zilēənt/

O backslider the Lord has not forgotten you. The Bible says,

"For it is impossible for those who were once enlightened, and have tasted of the heavenly gift, and were made partakers of the Holy Ghost, And have tasted the good word of God, and the powers of the world to come, If they shall fall away, to renew them again unto repentance; seeing they crucify to themselves the Son of GOD afresh, and put him to an open shame. (Hebrew 6:4-6)" With his outstretched arms he is saying to you, "Return, ye backsliding children, and I will heal your backslidings. Behold, we come unto thee; for thou art the Lord our God. (Jeremiah 3:22)", "Turn, O backsliding children, saith the Lord: for I am married unto you: and I will take you one of a city, and two of a family, and I will bring you to Zion: And I will give you pastors according to mine heart, which shall feed you with knowledge and understanding. (Jeremiah 3:13-15)" Backslider know that God's heart is always open to you. If we confess our sins He is faithful and just to forgive you.

As Bishop Marvin Winans sings, "I feel like going on, I feel like going on, though trials they may come on every hand. Oh I feel like going on Can I say I say it one more time? I feel like going on (I don't know how you feel about it) I feel like going on." Don't quit. Our challenges in life may knock us down but you can get up again and settle in your heart to stand in a spirit of faith, keep confessing and believing the word of GOD. No matter what it currently looks like quitting is not an option. Don't give up we are more than conquerors! "We are like common clay jars that carry this glorious treasure within, so that this immeasurable power will be seen as God's, not ours. Though we experience every kind of pressure, we're not crushed. At times we don't know what to do, but quitting is not an option. (2 Corinthians 4:7-9 The Passion Translation)"

Re·sil·ient
/rə'zilēənt/

I have found from all the trials, tribulations, disappointments and setbacks something good always comes from your journey. I thank Father God for the Holy Spirit. It is from the Holy Spirit that I gain my resilience. He is the one who gives me resurrection power not only for the future resurrection but he compels and empowers me to get back up again no matter how many times I've been knocked down. If you keep living you will find out life circumstances will knock you down. Rise up and count it all joy when you are down. It is the only way up in the kingdom of God. You can use this opportunity to evaluate the source of your strength and develop a closer relationship with your Father in heaven. He is the one who compels us and empowers us to keep believing, trusting, hoping and fighting the good fight of faith.

Scripture reference: Ephesians 1:19-20, James 1:2-4, Romans 8:28-31

Prayer: Today I pray to the Father in heaven that He will empower you with the Spirit of Resilience when your strength is depleted physically, spiritually, emotionally and mentally. I pray the Holy Spirit will give you His wisdom to know when to stop and breathe, to recharge and refuel with a new sound of worship and praise. I Decree and declare in the name of Jesus you shall rise up and your star shall shine and glorify GOD in the midst of adversity.

So it is and so shall it be in Jesus name

"Everyone who has been wise will shine as bright as the sky above, and everyone who has led others to please God will shine forever like the stars. (Daniel 12:3)"

Re·sil·ient
/rə'zilēənt/

These are a few testimonies of what the Lord has done for me. I hope you read these testimonies thinking Jesus is amazing. I want Him to come into my life too. I may not say everything in detail but I experienced the Power Of God. He is a healer and He is faithful. He answers my prayers. He guided me through every situation and gave me the victory. He talks with me through His word and shows me God's plan for my life. If you love Jesus and follow him with your whole heart Jesus will be your friend and never leave you.

On March 12, 2020 I was visiting my friends Beatrice and Barbara in Suwanee, Georgia. That evening after I ate I started feeling nauseous and vomited my food. I was not having any pain so I ignored it because my friends don't eat seasonal food for health reasons so to me the food tastes very bland. The next day I ate breakfast and later dinner and the same thing happened. Later that evening I started vomiting, sweating and became very light headed. That night my friend asked me if I was alright because she heard me vomiting and insisted I go to the emergency hospital. The next morning I was still in bed and she called my brother Orpheus Eugene in Atlanta and told him to come and take me to the emergency hospital because I would not go. I was admitted on March 15, 2020 into Emory Johns Creek Hospital emergency for pain on right side, nausea and vomiting. After extensive testing I was diagnosed with an acute appendicitis. When they entered the abdomen they found I had extremely thick phlegmon stuck to the right lower quadrant. The phlegmon was peeled off the abdominal wall revealing fecal contamination. Since there was intense inflammation in the area of the cecum and the appendix my doctor elected to do a partial appendectomy of the tip of the appendix.

Re·sil·ient
/rə'zilēənt/

If I had waited another day I may not be giving this testimony alive. But GOD who is faithful stops the assignment of the enemy to kill, steal and destroy my life. GOD said not so "she shall live and not die. I will live to recount the works of the Lord" (Psalm 118:17) I was discharged on March 16, 2020. My life is safe in his hands and I am still alive to tell what the Lord has done for me.

May 4, 2020 I kept feeling dizzy, light headed and fainting for several days. On this morning I passed out on the kitchen floor and when I woke up my mother saw me and she panic and I told her to call the police for an ambulance. They took me to St Joseph/Candler emergency. They took all kinds of tests and could not find the problem. The doctor diagnoses me with epilepsy and syncope, The doctor prescribed Levetiracetam for epilepsy and an opioid pill for pain. I didn't know at the time what I was taking but I started hallucinating, anxious, mood swings and I was acting crazy. Thank GOD I had surrounded myself with praying people and people of faith ".....and calleth those things which be not as though they were. (Roman 4:17)" If you smell death in the room they will say "you shall not die but live to declare the works of the Lord (Psalms 118:17)". I stopped taking the medication after reading about the side effects. The diagnosis was a lie from the pit of hell. The devil was after my mind. He couldn't kill my body now he wants to destroy my mind. But God said in His word "No weapon formed against me shall prosper" (Isaiah 54:17)" The doctor called my son Oscar A. Greene III and asked him if I was religious. He asked him why he said it because she is in the hospital talking about Jesus and calling his name.

They sent a nun in my room to talk to me and I thought to myself "Am I going to die"? After our conversation, you know what happened? She left the room more confused about who she was serving. God gave me the grace to witness to her, the doctors, nurses, interns, nutritionist and everybody that came into the room. The word was out on the floor and in the hospital that this woman was crazy because all she talked about is Jesus. If I didn't call on the name of Jesus I would have been dead and in a grave. I never would have survived. On May 8, 2020 I was discharged and again still here to testify.

On May 4 thru May 8, 2022: My God did it again. The enemy wanted to sift me like wheat but my God , Jesus prayed for me. (Luke 22:31-32) I was admitted in the emergency at St Joseph's Candler Hospital and test were taken and I was diagnosed with acute cholecystitis, a severely inflamed gallbladder, dense scarring hard thickened omentum surrounding the gallbladder, dense scarring around the neck of the gallbladder, cystic duct and cystic artery and hard stone filling entire neck of gallbladder. This was quite tedious and the procedure took longer than usual. I needed prayer and GOD sent a prayer warrior and intercessor name Yolanda Ford-Mitchell who called my pastors Bishop James and Dr Phyllis RODGES to pray. My pastors touch the heart of God and the heavens opened. The prophetic prayer warrior Yolanda kept praying and stayed in the hospital with me because we knew this fight was not natural, it was spiritual. Well we won with the help of the Holy Spirit. Today I am healed and testifying "God will and God can do anything but fail"

Re·sil·ient
/rə'zilēənt/

To the person reading this, commit yourself to the only true and living God! Give your life to the Lord Jesus Christ, and surrender everything to Him. HE gave His only Son to us that we may have life and enjoy it. ....."But I have come to give you everything in abundance, more than you expect—life in its fullness until you overflow!" (John 10:10 The Passion Translation)

Do not fear because He is a faithful God!

Re·sil·ient
/rəˈzilēənt/

Questions

1. Do you qualify to testify?

2. I bought a journal by Pastor Rick titled
"It"s not cheap to be you."

Are you willing to pay the price?

3. What is your true testimony?

4. Why should you testify?

If you know God as your heavenly Father;
Jesus Christ as your Savior and Redeemer,
knowledge of the word of God, compassion, humility,
obedience, and faith in what you believe then you qualify to
testify and bring others to Him.

I love you!

Re·sil·ient
/rə'zilēənt/

Journaling

Re·sil·ient
/rə'zilēənt/

Journaling

Re·sil·ient
/rə'zilēənt/

Journaling

REV. NATHANIEL EUGENE HOLSEY
The Fourteenth Pastor
1943 ~ 1947

Rev. Nathaniel E. Holsey succeeded Rev. L.M. Terrill as Pastor of First Bryan Baptist Church. Though he did not remain for a long period of time, a great deal was accomplished.

He was married and there were three children. Mrs. Bennie Holsey, (second wife) was a popular soloist. They came to First Bryan from Arkansas. Rev. Holsey was a dynamic Preacher and Evangelist. The Members liked him very much. Shortly after becoming Pastor, he helped with planning and erection of the addition at the rear of the church, which created space for the bathrooms, choir room, anteroom and the present choir stand, back of the pulpit. Originally the anteroom was used for counting offerings. During his Pastorate, a Baby Grand and Hammond Organ was purchased, because the organ upstairs ceased to function. It was then that the choir also moved to the present location, back of the pulpit.

The Holsey's celebrated their twenty-fifth Wedding Anniversary in the church.

Rev. Nathaniel Holsey resigned after four years to accept the call to a church in Philadelphia, Pa. He returned twice and preached at First Bryan.

Re·sil·ient

/rə'zilēənt/

Reverend Nathaniel Holsey was an innovator, a civil rights activist, a true servant of God. He previously was Pastor of Union Springs Baptist, Hot Springs, Arkansas. While there he was president of the Interdenominational Ministers Alliance, musical director of the Southwest District Sunday School, BTU, and Usher Board Congress; a board member of the Southwest District.

He was also a nationally known evangelist, as well as a member of the educational board of the National Baptist Convention. He became the 14th Pastor of First Bryan in 1943. He preached his initial sermon on September 24th, 1943. My brother is also named after our grandfather.

Re·sil·ient
/rə'zilēənt/

Rev. Nathaniel E. Holsey a Georgia native, attended Morehouse College, and received his baccalaureate degree from Western College in St. Louis. During his first year as Pastor First Bryan Celebrated it's 156th Anniversary January 16 - 20, 1944. The first 6 months of his pastorate in which the following were accomplished: a new baby grand piano, purchased and paid for a new microphone system installed and the lighting system improved.

On September 8th, 1945 he delivered the evangelistic sermon at the National Baptist Convention in Detroit, Michigan as he was a noted evangelist and revivalist in national Baptist church circles. From November 18 - 26, 1945, a dedicatory service was held for Reverend Holsey in recognition of his progressive two year leadership which included extensive renovations to the church building.

Under his leadership, in October, 1946 First Bryan began weekly Sunday night broadcasts over WDAR radio which included sermonettes by Reverend Holsey and renditions by the church chior. He was the first minister at First Bryan to pioneer live remote radio broadcast programs from the church through WDAR.

When Reverend Holsey resigned in June 1949 it signaled the close of an era at the church. Jim Crow, racism, lack of political and social rights for blacks were the order of the day throughout the history of First Bryan

Re·sil·ient
/rə'zilēənt/

Mr. and Mrs. Holsey 25th Wedding Anniversary at
First Bryan Baptist Church

Re·sil·ient

/rə'zilēənt/

I recently learned about all my grandfather Rev. Nathaniel E. Holsey accomplishments and the Godly heritage in my family bloodline. God definitely had a plan as he did with Jesus protecting the seed down to 42 generations. I am honored to follow in his foot steps. Our steps are definitely ordered by the Lord.

"The steps of the God-pursuing ones follow firmly in the footsteps of the Lord. And God delights in every step they take to follow Him. Psalm 37:23 (The Passion Translations)"

Re·sil·ient
/rə'zilēənt/

For more stories about Reverend Holsey and First Bryan Baptist Church, you can purchase the book below by Charles J. Elmore.

Re·sil·ience (rə'zilyəns) noun 1. the capacity to recover quickly from difficulties; toughness. 2. the ability of an object to spring back

My Declarations

Chapter 6
My Declarations

This Year I decree And Declare In Jesus Name That:

I am saved

I am delivered

I am healed

I am happy

I am healthy and I am whole.

I have understanding, and wisdom

I will receive abundantly above all that I may ask or think, according to the power that is working in me.

I can do great things because I can do all things through Christ, who strengthens me.

Our Father in Heaven remembers His promises and He is bringing you to your expected end so you can have hope and a future

When The righteous cry the Lord answers
NO WEAPON, NO WEAPON, NO WEAPON will prevent God's plan from coming forth in the lives of His Children

Destiny and Purpose have kissed!

1-3 Thank you! Everything in me says "Thank you!"
Angels listen as I sing my thanks. I kneel in worship facing your holy temple and say it again: "Thank you!" Thank you for your love, thank you for your faithfulness; Most holy is your name, most holy is your Word. The moment I called out, you stepped in; you made my life large with strength.
4-6 When they hear what you have to say, God, all earth's kings will say "Thank you." They'll sing of what you've done:"How great the glory of God And here's why: God, high above, sees far below; no matter the distance, he knows everything about us.
Psalm 138:1-6 (The Message Bible)

"Religion is only one expression of spiritual resilience. Spiritual resilience is found in the ability to sustain an individual's sense of self and purpose through their beliefs, principles, values and morals. It is not only about how we recover from adversity. Additionally, spiritual resilience is shaped in how we bounce back/rebound through difficulties and move forward within deeper knowledge of both God and ourselves.... Your spiritual resilience is the ability to maintain a positive spirit even in the face of adversity.... Spiritual resilience is not about religion, its about how you find meaning in life; what keeps you grounded and where you find purpose. Through each life experience, we engage in soul seeking for identity and connection. Spiritual resilience can be defined by how we live out our faith. It is learned as we experience life and all that it brings.... Spiritual Resilience enables us to be spiritually led, not emotional responders."

THE WORD ~ Jesus answered them, "Do you finally believe? In fact, you're about to make a run for it-saving your own skins and abandoning me. But I'm not abandoned. The Father is with me. I've told you all this so that trusting me, you will be unshakable and assured, deeply at peace.

SPIRITUAL RESILIENCE - Dr. Sarita Wilson-Guffin
Director, Spiritual Care Le Bonheur Children's Hospital

"In this godless world you will continue to experience difficulties. But take heart! I've conquered the world. (John 16:31-33 MSG)"

Remember some of you have not reached your destiny yet, but you're giving birth. The labour pains are intense. You've got to push. You must learn to walk by faith, and live by faith. As your Apostolic Spiritual Midwife I say PUSH BABY PUSH! You are about to step into your destiny. You are closer to your destiny than you were yesterday. Because of your resilience, your faithfulness and in spite of everything that was against you, here comes destiny.

God is about to reward you. Some of you are walking in destiny ,your dreams and visions have come to pass. You have transformed from a caterpillar to a butterfly. You are becoming who God said you would become and going places and doing things he declared you would do. Reach back and grab your sister or brothers hand and encourage them to push and step into their destiny. Tell them the truth, this is your greatest moment. The things you are going through is preparing you for greatness. Push, you are unstoppable, Push don't let the storms of life stop you from your progress. Push your times has come. The trials and tribulations, the persecution and afflictions are elevators to take you higher.

"And we know that all things work together for good to them that love God, to them who are the called according to his purpose. (Romans 8:28)"

Evangelist Deborius Greene

You Are Invited

If you are not born again (John 3:5-7) and you would like to surrender your life to Jesus the Christ, you can do so right now, right there where you are, all you need to do is acknowledge that you are a sinner, repent of your sins; confess them to the Lord and ask him to forgive you. Renounce your sins and decide that your mind's made up and you won't go back to them anymore. I applaud you for this decision that you have made it is the best and most important decision in life. Pray this prayer with faith and sincerity.

Father in the name of Jesus I repent of all my sins and I believe in Jesus Christ as my Savior and his blood that was shed for the cleansing of my sins. I surrender and yield my life completely to the Lord Jesus. I want to live a pure and holy life. I invite the powerful overcoming blood of Jesus into every area of my life. Lord you know me better than i know myself you know the emotional pain that I have been going through, the open wounds that are still bleeding and the anguish inside of me. I come to you Lord to heal my emotions, heal my wounded heart and heal the deep anguish inside of me. Oh Lord come into my heart and bind up the brokenness within me. Lord let your healing love flood into every dark place of my being. Root out all the negative emotions with the fire and the blood of Jesus in Jesus name. You are my shepherd and I am trusting you to release into every void within me your love, your peace, your hope and your presence. I speak your words "thou wilt shew me the path of life: in thy presence is fullness of joy; at thy right hand there are pleasures for evermore" (Psalms 16:11). Lord I know that your word says that you will give strength to the weary and hope to the distressed, I need your help and strength, you promised in Isaiah 40:29-31) that those who wait on the Lord you will renew their strength

and rise up with wings of eagles. Help me to wait on you. Help me to abide in you and rest in your love. Heal my broken heart and restore unto me the joy of my salvation. Help me to stop thinking about the painful memories of the past. Help me to let it go and concentrate on the great future you have planned for me. Help me to be more like Jesus. Help me to forgive those that have hurt me and deliver me from resentments. Take away the bitter feelings of anger and betrayal inside me, teach me how to love others in the same way that Jesus loves me and gave his life for me. Thank you for your promise to heal the brokenhearted and restore those that are hurting (Psalms 147:3) Thank you Jesus for answered prayers. Amen!

I love you

63

It embodies resilience, as rain from dark clouds slides easily off its petals and it opens itself to the sunshine that follows.

This uniquely beautiful plant only grows in the mud and has the ability to be reborn every day; At night, the flower closes and submerges under the water, and at dawn emerges and reopens splendidly

No one's ever seen or heard anything like this,
Never so much as imagined anything quite like it—
What God has arranged for those who love him.
But you've seen and heard it because God by his Spirit has brought it all out into the open before you.

1 Corinthians 2:9 (The Message Bible)

All Scripture References Taken From:

The King James Bible
The Message Bible
Contemporary English Version
English Standard Version
The Passion Translation

Information about Reverend Nathaniel E. Holsey taken from "First Bryan" by Charles J. Elmore

Printed by Kindle Direct Publishing

First printing, 2023

Jana Hicks Publishing
New York